Deja Vu with Food

From my Grandmother's Kitchen

Written, Compiled & Food Styling

By Nevedita Kharbanda

ISBN
Paperback 979-8-89632-975-6
Hardcase 979-8-89673-384-3

Déjà vu with Food...

Food has the ability to transport us to different times, places and connect us with our traditions, family, and roots!

From my grandmother's kitchen

Deja vu with food...

Written, designed, compiled & Food styling by Nevedita Kharbanda

To Marvellous Ashish & Neil...

Memories of a specific dish, food or flavour can evoke powerful feelings of comfort and security, often bringing up happy memories of times spent with friends and family...

Contents

Introduction

Introduction

The Shade of Tree, Fruit & Family

Today when I cook food for family, friends, festivals or travel it transports me back to my childhood. It brings back a myriad of memories. Each meal, each dish transports me back to the place that was home. Every season, every vegetable, every aroma, every tree, the flowers that bloom in different seasons, bring back memories. We live in cities now. Every time I visit a vegetable or fruit market, every seasonal change transports me back to the people and place. When I am reading about food with my 8-year-old son, I start telling him how the Jamun tree looks, how aromatic a ripe jackfruit is, it smells and tastes like custard.

The litchi, mango, guava orchards not only give us fruit but shade too. Playing around the trees, with cousins hanging on the branches during summer vacations, eating and plucking the fresh fruit brings back multitude of memories. The happiness of looking at the litchi bunch hanging on a tree, trying to pluck them by jumping, eating, and playing around it. Family get togethers, bon-fires, singing, playing hide & seek hanging on the trees. The shade of the tree & family is irreplaceable.

We had different varieties of flowers in the garden. Red roses blooming would become edible when used in decorating kheer or making gulkand. Sitting under the Jackfruit tree and kitchen garden discussing different recipes, our chulha was right under the mango tree in the angaan. The smokey flavour of chulhe ki roti,with fresh white butter is the best memory I have. With an abundance of harvest even house help contributed to create recipes including me.

I am the eldest & first grandchild of the family loved very dearly by the entire family. Being the only child till other children were born my journey with food began without me even knowing how much I breathe food. My Grandfather was an IAS officer. We got the opportunity to live in big bungalows with a big kitchen garden, mango, litchi, jamun, jackfruit, peaches and narangi trees around.

A big joint family, my dad being the eldest. My grandmother who made the delicious food I would say even if she would touch the utensil, it would bring out flavours, aromas which I till now can smell and taste. Men in my family cooked from my grandfather to my dad to all the uncles though we had so much house help they all loved creating recipes, it was like an in house food event happening all the time.

Our kitchen garden was always loaded with fresh vegetables, ladyfingers, potatoes, papaya, meethi, spinach saag, fresh coriander and mint leaves were grown in abundance, so garnishing a dish with freshest leaves was a must. Menu revolved around what was growing. It was a farm to table meal on an everyday basis.

1

Living in a joint family gave me an opportunity to learn from everyone, my grandparents, parents, aunts, and uncles. I was introduced to global food or cuisine at an early childhood thanks to my family. Living in different geographies in India, Uttar Pradesh being my birthplace, I have travelled a lot with my grandparents and after getting married got the opportunity to experience the beautiful culture, food, and people from the states of Uttarakhand, Punjab, and Karnataka. Our country is truly a land of diversity.

Dehradun (Uttarakhand rain and cloud reminds me of 'maggi aur chai' at maggi point. I learnt to cook the local food kulath dal (horse gram dal, Phanoo a rustic hearty, black urad Garhwali dal and Gulguley sweet pue made with banana and atta mixture during special occasions. Camping & Bonfire in Rishikesh on the bank of river Ganga would take me back to the childhood bonfires and cooking.

My Grandparents belonged to Agra (Uttar Pradesh). The best chaat I would remember is from Agra beside it being famous for Petha (sweet). It is difficult to say whether Dilli ki chaat or Uttar Pradesh ki chaat which one is better. Both bring back a plethora of memories & taste.

Living in Bengaluru (Karnataka), I was introduced to a different cuisine. I was introduced to Ragi the amazing super food that is part of our daily meals now. Delhi is the heart of not just the country but food too.

Delhi is the heart of foodies. My most transformative years began when I came to Delhi for my graduation at 'Lady Shri Ram College.' I owe a lot to this place. Living in the hostel has a special bonding not just with the friends we make for life but with the food too, it is etched in life to cherish forever. Our college canteen had delicious macaroni with cheese, kathi rolls, dosa, chai and sandwiches. Whenever i try to make these recipes for my son i am transported back by the taste, aroma and look of it to the college canteen.

We all love to travel, road travels to any city are a unique experience. Every village, every farm, every tree, the Moon, the Sun, the Stars, people, and the food has a different feel. We get to eat the best highway Dhaba food. Punjab travels are our favourite. It is a foodie paradise dal makhani,white butter, choley kulche, lassi, butter chicken, fish, saag. The swirls of ghee tadka on dal and kadhi reminds me of grandmother's cooking. It is delicious. Whenever I try to recreate these recipes, the aroma and taste just transports me back. It is a deja vu.

***Food is music to the body
much like music is food
to the heart.***

The Verandah & Angan

The Verandah has become a vintage thing, a thing of a beautiful past gone by. Sadly, we do not design them this is where i have spent my innumerable childhood. This is where we enjoyed rain, sun, air, food straight from dadimaa's chulha.

It depicted everything warm, cosy, simple, beautiful, and soul stirring. You ate here and listened to stories by dadi, chacha chachis, old fans with long rods, the cane woven bed and chairs. The recipes were decided for evenings in the verandah and angan.

The Angan and veranda was always shining with pickle jars, golden drops of vadi drying in the sun. Everything was pickled mango, jackfruit, lemon, red and green chillies in the Angan. I still make vadi's and pickles at home, but the Angan has squeezed to the balconies of an apartment. My son loves to help me make the vadi's & pickles.

In the evening, the fruit of labour was relished by the entire family. With singing around the chulha, food and music have been two inseparable things for our family. My dad played mouth organ with Hemant Kumar songs being his all-time favourite, my uncles, aunts played different instruments drums, guitar, harmonium, and everyone sang together including my grandfather & Grandmother. Food creates bonding & the deja vu continues.

<u>*Pandemic & Food*</u>

As a saying goes *'We have two lives, and the second begins when we realise, we only have one.'*

We all have been through a phase where we were trying recipes, taking pictures, sharing on social media. There was food all over. But there was another side to it, the pandemic had taken away a lot of loved ones' family & friends. We were hit by it too. God has been kind to have given us another chance to appreciate life.

This is exactly when my journey to healthy eating, exercising & following my passion started. My husband & I promised to take care of ourselves, so we can take care of our son. When we started eating healthy, we realised we are going back to basics, all the millets, jowar, bajra, ragi, kodo, lentils & sprouts. Fermented food like gajar kanji, idli and dosas. Bel sharbat, raw turmeric milk, makhana to jowar popcorn. We were eating what my grandmother used to make and eat.

Cooking the same dishes, it is therapeutic. Food heals inside out.
I tried to recreate my grandmother's dahi gujiya recipe into a healthier version of steamed dahi gujiya.

During the lockdown i got the opportunity to do a cook along for my college alumni Lady Shriram college Bengaluru Chapter. We created recipes for 'ELSA table.'
It was an enriching experience. I learned a lot from my seniors and batch mates. Each one shared their family recipes.

"*Cooking is like painting or writing a song. Just as there are only so many notes or colours, there are only so many flavours—it is how you combine them that sets you apart.*"

– Wolfgang Puck

I had authored a poem, an ode to food.

Main roz aisi ek nayi kavita banana chahti hu…

Smita ne kaha abhi 11 din hai baaki
Kuch likhne ka prayaas karo nevi…

Mainey socha chalo kuch likhtey hai
Dil ki baat ko siyahi mein dibotey hai…

Par korey kagaz par
siyahi se na likh payi

Phir socha canvas par lakirey kachtey hai
Shayaad kavita ban jaye, par nahi ba payi…

Phir maine apni kavita banayi
Sab ke saat thaali mein parosi
Mehkti hui si, Ruh ko chu lene wali
Hanstey hue, jhoomtey hue
Kavita parosi…

Naam nahi meri kavita ka koi
Baas angaan ko mehaka de
Mushkurahat lade, Ruh ko sukoon diladey
Aur pyaar baatey hue

Main,
Roz ek aisi nayi kavita
Banana chahaati hun…

Jo har mausam, har ritu, har din
Kabhi meethi si, kabhi khatti si, kabhi teekhi si
Yaadoon ka carvaan buntey hue
Hamesha ke liye
Ruh ko chu jaye
Main
Roz ek aisi nayi kavita banana chahti hu…
6th April 2021

MARVELOUS
Mrs India
MMI 2
#BeautyInsideOut
DR. ADITI GOVITRIKAR
DIRECTOR/ FOUNDER
tathastu

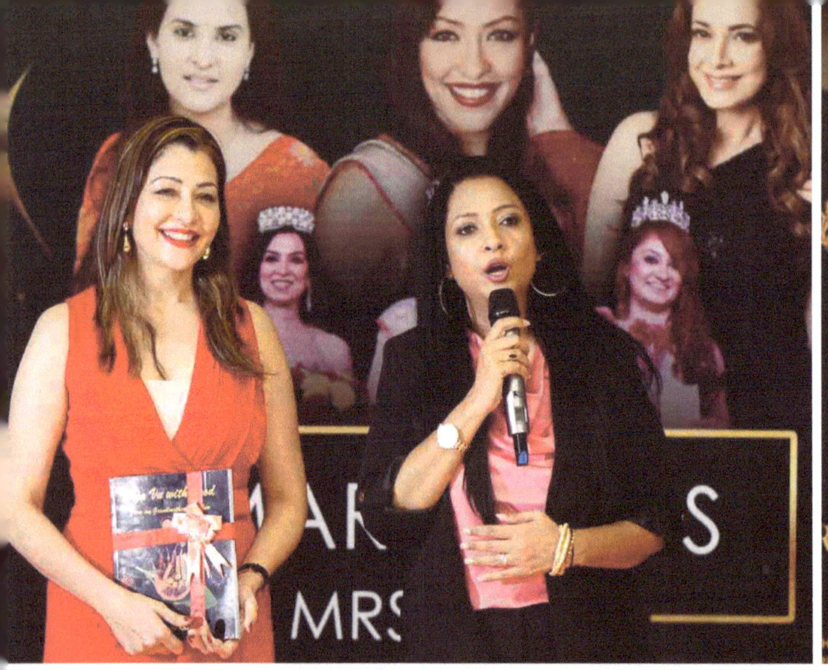

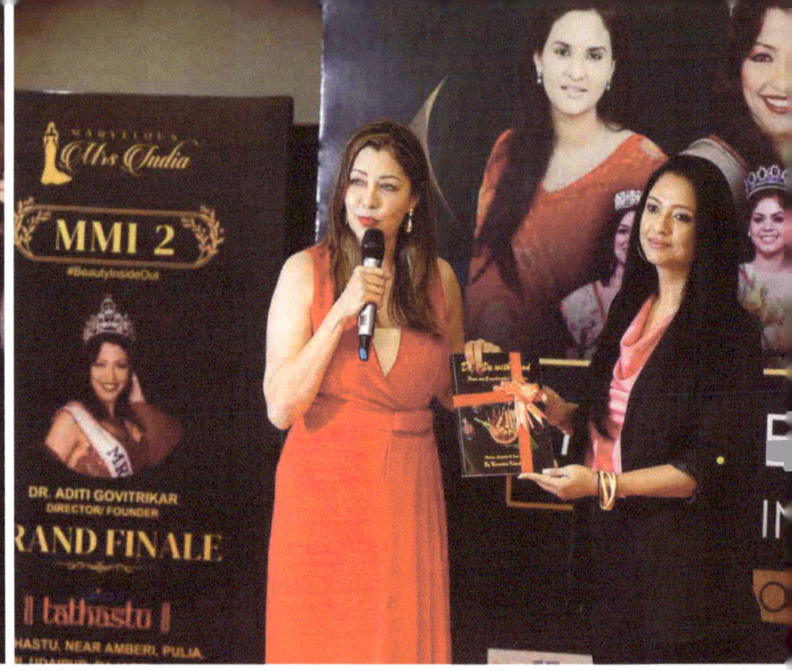

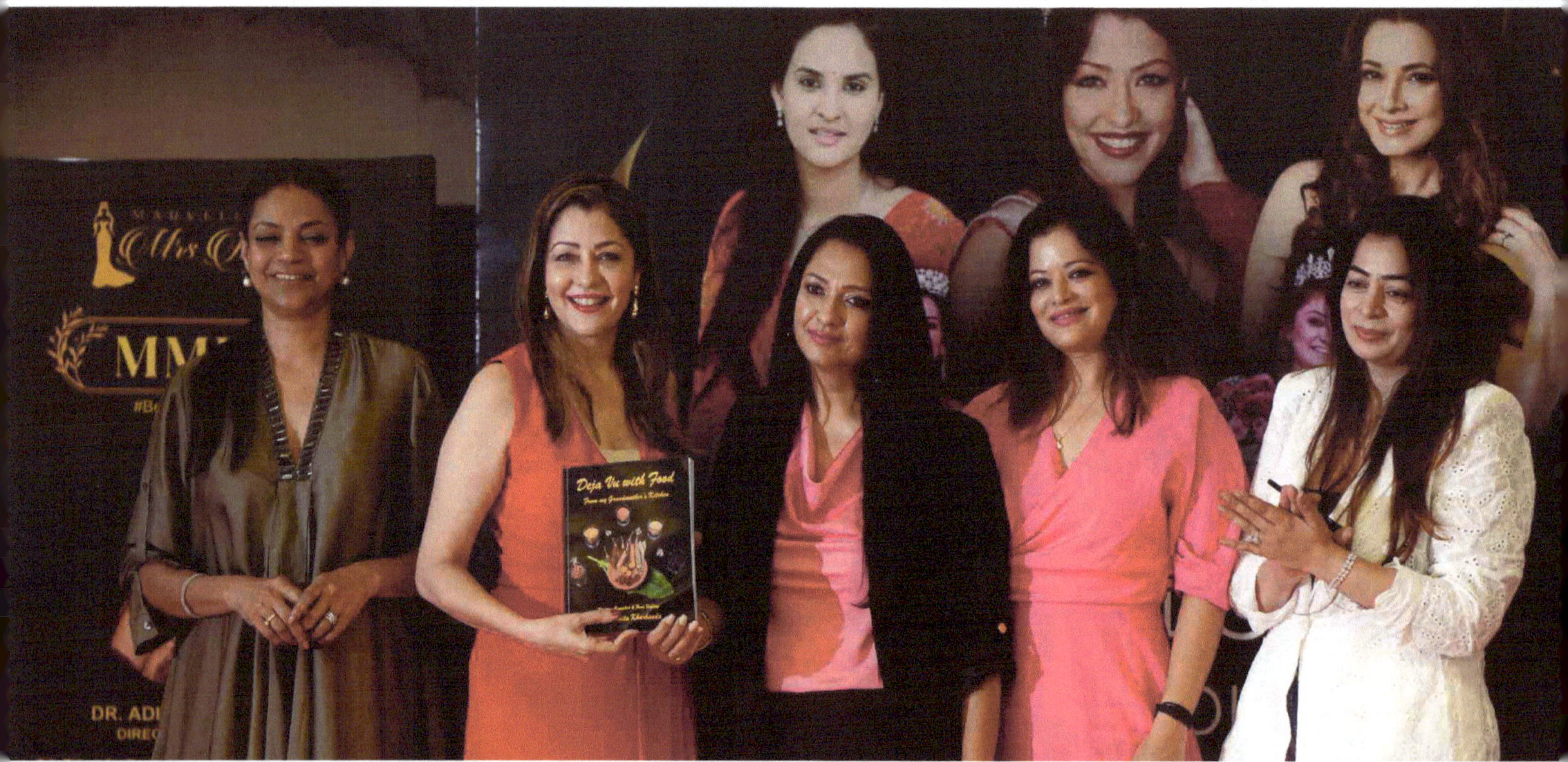
Deja Vu with Food
From my Grandmother's Kitchen

MARVELOUS

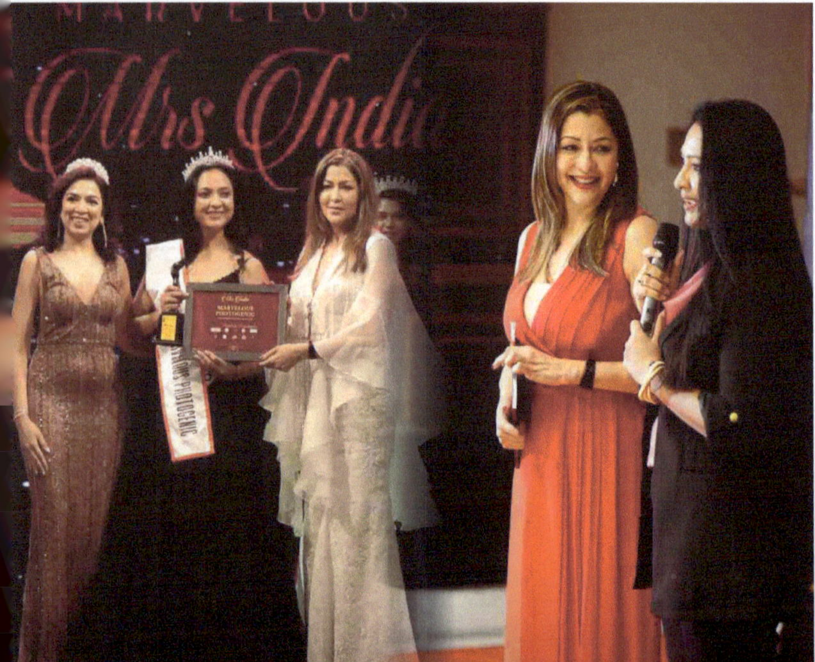

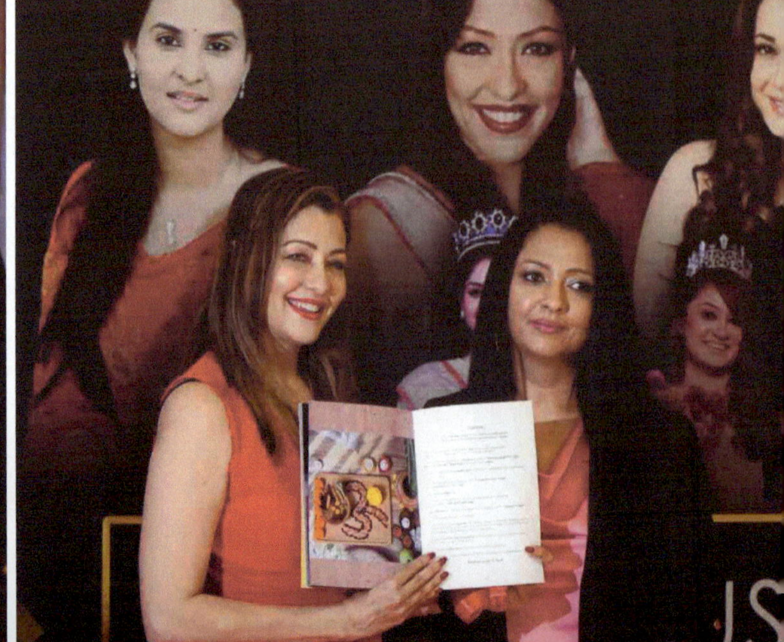

<u>*Marvellous Journey from Food to Heels*</u>

Food when offered to God becomes Prasadam,
Food when eaten in a balanced way transforms you…
Food is the fuel for every living being on the planet…
Food brings people together…
Food does not discriminate…

Food made me wear heels,
Food is glamorous…
The journey of self-Discovery … Pageantry!

MARVELOUS
Mrs India
MMI 2

MARVELOUS
Mrs India
MARVELOUS
PHOTOGENIC
MARVELOUS PHOTOGENIC

MARVELOUS PHOTO
26

I started with a weight loss journey transformation while eating home cooked healthy balanced meals. Gym,exercising and strength training, from not knowing how to walk on a treadmill or workout in the gym, to lifting weights. It helps a person not only to be independent physically but mentally for a longer time. It helped me through my darkest and most challenging times.

During the journey, my husband had a brain stroke which shook me and my son badly. We bought the heels together and he had to see me wear them on the beautiful milestone of ,25th year of our marriage. The book was yet to be completed. I had to write, cook food, click pictures, design the cover and complete the book. I had to juggle with so many roles from being a caregiver to my husband, a mother to my 8 year old son, running around between home & hospital somewhere in between all this, I tried to write the book but it needed more time.

 I believe women are truly the embodiment of Shakti, we have immense strength within, we just need to find out the true potential. For me to participate in Pageantry or complete the book seemed impossible. I am blessed to have the most progressive men in my life from my Dad, husband to my son. My husband motivated me to finish what I started. God has been kind to us. Due to the Brain stroke my husband couldn't walk properly without support. Once my husband was discharged from the hospital we both started to learn how to walk. He started with his physiotherapy and I learnt how to walk in heels. The track was the same inside our living room. We tried to support each other and walk everyday together.

I had to finish my book, being a caregiver, mother and preparing for a pageant in between somewhere I cooked for 3 days & nights continuously. I was only smelling of food. The entire house was loaded with food as I had to take pictures for the recipes. My husband was on medication so he couldn't even taste what I cooked. Cooking is therapeutic. I found peace while cooking that I am so passionate about. Finally the dining table was set for the photo shoot, with all the food that I had cooked. We thought we would buy some fancy tableware, glassware, cutlery and decor. But God had other plans. I was running short of time so whatever I had at home I used it for taking pictures. When my husband was discharged from the hospital we got a small puja and havan done at home to thank God. I never knew it would become the cover of my book. It was the first picture that I clicked with the camera. We always used to discuss how the book cover would be. This is how the book cover was created. My heart is filled with Gratitude to God. It was not easy but with the support of my loved ones I was able to complete the book.

Dr Aditi Govitrikar is the director of the pageant Marvelous Mrs India. Dr Aditi was crowned as the first Mrs World from India. She has a doctor's degree in psychology. Dr Aditi has been with us throughout the most challenging times from praying to being with us rock solid. From guiding how to walk in heels, motivating me with the strength training in the gym, to being the guiding force behind writing a book that I passionately wanted to write.

The day arrived when I had to leave for the pageant. This time hoping to see both of them soon ,my husband and son at the pageant that was to be held in, Udaipur. My husband had not stepped out of the house besides visiting the doctors in the hospital. We thought we all would travel together for the pageant, to the beautiful city of lakes, Udaipur. We had visited, Udaipur for the new year in the year 2023.Sometimes some places one visits mean something more than we think. The city was calling again but this time it was different.

I packed my bags, with two bags full of books. The book was to be launched at the pageant. I gathered my strength, prayed to God and went to, Udaipur. I was physically in, Udaipur but mentally I was with my husband & son. I reached the venue. I met the most wonderful people, each contestant a true queen & inspiring. It was not at all a competition, rather felt like a function where you meet your extended family. All the sister queens were amazing. I met my mentor Dr. Aditi in person for the first time. She is a true queen. Truly beauty with brains and a marvelous human being. I met my mentor for the ramp walk Ms.Nayanika Chatterjee in person super- talented & a marvelous human being. My journey from food to heels began. Time was moving fast & I was keeping my fingers crossed to meet my family on the finale day.

On the 11th of October we entered the beautiful milestone of the 25th year of our marriage. I was in, Udaipur this was the day my book was launched at the Pageant by Dr.Aditi Govitrikar. I never thought I would be wearing heels for the 25th year of our marriage and getting my first culinary book launched. God has his own plans.
The Pageant finale day arrived. After visiting the doctor and getting a go ahead to travel my husband and son took the flight from Delhi to Udaipur. My 8 year old son was the father now and my husband was the son now. My son helped his dad reach Udaipur. I had not met them until now.

On the finale night, wearing my heels, I stepped on the ramp looking for my husband and son among the audience. We all love Bollywood and this day was my 'Bollywood moment' among the audience while walking the ramp wearing my heels i see my son & husband to my left, i see my mentors to my right Dr. Aditi Govitrikar & Ms. Nayanika Chatterjee and the esteemed judges sitting right in the centre Ms. Neelam Kothari and chief guest Maharaj Kunwarani Sahiba Nivithri kumari Mewar , in my mind a thought entered, i thought to myself & God, "we all wear so many invisible crown, this **'moment'** is my crown."

I was crowned as **MarvelousMrsPhotogenic.** While getting crowned in most photographs instead of looking towards the camera I was looking towards my family. I never knew the journey I had embarked on would really help me pass through the storm. God has been kind. Marvelousness truly lies within each one of us. We just sometimes need someone to bring out the best in us and make us believe in ourselves.
My healthy eating habits really helped me during the recovery phase of my husband. The moment he was handed over with a diet chart, I was not puzzled at all. Food is fuel to recovery if eaten in a balanced & healthy way.
Writing this book is part of the marvelous journey. I always wanted to share and preserve the recipes which my grandmother & family have relished. To the future generations, my son who would know where all the food in me has come from, I want to leave it as a legacy for my son. Food and kitchen are emotions of togetherness & memories. Health is something that cannot be bought.
Cooking is a life skill that everyone should learn. Hope one day my son cooks a heartful meal and enjoys it with his own family and remembers every aroma, every taste, and the Deja vu will continue with food. At the end it is a circle of life.
Hiraeth (Welsh word } a home or place we can never return to, trying to recreate these for ourselves and our children on special occasions, with every dish that has a story, emotion, and a Deja vu.

<u>**_Family Recipes_**</u>

Family is the most important ingredient in the recipe of life, here are a few recipes from my grandmother's kitchen.

Family Recipes

Turai ke chilke ke kebab

Prep time: 30 minutes
Cookout time: 20 minutes
Serves: 4
Storage: Refrigerate (can be stored for 2 to 3 days)
Utensils Required -Pressure cooker, Non-stick tawa for shallow frying, spatula & deep bowl for mixing.
For Plating: Plate/ tray

Ingredients

- ½ kg Ridge gourd peels
- 1 cup-soaked Chana dal
- 1 small piece Ginger
- 4 cloves Garlic
- 1 chopped onion
- Finely chopped green chillies
- Finely chopped fresh mint leaves
- Finely chopped fresh coriander leaves
- Whole spices (cinamon1/2, 4 cloves, 1 big black cardamom, 2 small green cardamom)
- Salt to taste
- Vegetable oil or Pomace olive oil or Desi Ghee for shallow frying

Instructions

1. Soak chana dal for 30 minutes.
2. Wash the ridge gourd peels in running water and soak them in hot water for 10 minutes.
3. Pressure cook all the ingredients for 3 whistles.
4. Add little water while pressure cooking.
5. Cool and grind them.
6. Add finely chopped onions, fresh coriander leaves, mint leaves, lime juice, salt to taste and pepper powder.
7. Shape them into round patties and shallow fry on a nonstick tawa.
8. Serve hot with mint coriander chutney.

Note Can be Air fried.

Soya shammi Kebab (veg)

Prep time: 30 minutes
Cookout time: 20 minutes
Serves: 4
Storage: Refrigerate (can be stored for 2 to 3 days)
Utensils Required
Pressure cooker, Nonstick Tawa, Spatula and Deep Bowl for mixing
For Plating: Plate/ tray

Ingredient List

- 150 gms soya nuggets chunks required
- 1 cup channa Dal
- ½ inch of ginger
- 15 to 20 cloves Garlic
- Whole garam masala (1 tsp jeera, 1 small stick cinnamon, 2 black
- cardamom, 2 green cardamoms, 2 bay leaves, 5 to 6 black peppercorns, 4 cloves)
- 2 whole dry red chilli
- Freshly chopped coriander
- 1 medium onion finely chopped
- 3 tsp freshly chopped mint leaves
- 2 green chillies chopped
- ½ tsp red chilli powder (optional)
- Salt to taste
- Oil for shallow frying (vegetable or pomace olive oil)

Instructions

1. Soak Soya nugget chunks for 15 minutes in hot water, wash under running water thoroughly, squeeze out water from nuggets.
2. Soak chana dal for 10 minutes.
3. In a pressure cooker add squeezed soya chunks, soaked chana dal, whole garam masala, whole red chillies, garlic, ginger, 1 tsp of salt add 3 cups of water, after 1 whistle lower the flame let it cook for 15 minutes.
4. Open the cooker, strain the mixture, and let the excess water strain thru the strainer at least for an hour. (leave it for an hour we get dry mixture)
5. Once the excess water is strained grind the mixture in the grinder (not very smooth it should be coarse)
6. Transfer the mixture to a bowl add chopped onions, fresh coriander, fresh mint leaves, green chilies, salt to taste and mix well.
7. Divide the mixture into equal round shaped kebabs.
8. Heat the non-stick tawa, drizzle 2 to 3 tsp oil place the kebabs on it, cook both the sides. Cook till Golden brown.
9. Serve with mint coriander chutney

Tip/ Special care

Let the mixture strain excess water thru the stainer for at least an hour
Do not soak chana dal for more than 10 minutes.
Wash the soya nuggets after soaking for 15 minutes under running
Water.

Sweet Potato Beetroot Sattu Cutlet

Prep time: 30 minutes
Cookout time: 20 minutes
Serves: 4
Storage: Refrigerate (can be stored for 2 to 3 days)
Utensils Required -Pressure cooker, Non-Stick Tawa for shallow frying, spatula & deep bowl for mixing.
For Plating: Plate/ tray

Ingredient List

- 2 to 3 Boiled sweet potato
- 1 beetroot grated
- 1 finely Chopped onion
- ½ inch Ginger
- Fresh Green coriander finely chopped
- Fresh finely chopped Mint
- 1 Spring onion greens finely chopped
- 1 tbsp Flax seed powder
- 3 to 4 tbsp Sattu for binding
- 1 Lemon juice
- Salt to taste
- ½ tsp Pepper
- ½tsp Jeera powder
- ½ tsp Garam masala

Instructions

1. Boil sweet potato and beet in a pressure cooker.
2. Cool, peel and mash the sweet potato in a mixing bowl, add grated boiled beetroot.
3. Add fresh coriander leaves chopped, mint leaves and only green leaves of the spring onion.
4. Add 1 tbsp of flaxseed powder.
5. Add 3 to 4 tbsp of sattu powder for binding.
6. Squeeze a juice of 1 lemon, ginger, ½ tsp garam masala, ½ tsp of jeera powder, ½ tsp pepper and salt to taste.
7. Mix well, make round patties, shallow fry them on both the sides.
8. Serve hot with fresh mint and coriander chutney.

Note : Can also be Air fried.

Stuffed Dahi Gujiya (Festival Special Holi and Diwali)

- Prep time: 4 hours
- Cooking Time: 20 to 25 minutes
- Serves: 6
- Storage: Refrigerate
- Utensils Required:
- Heavy bottomed Kadai
- Deep bowl/dish for soaking
- Deep bowl/disposable leaf bowl/donga for plating

Ingredients

- 200 gms (1 Cup) Split Urad dal
- ½ tsp salt
- 25 -30 Raisins
- Finely chopped dry coconut
- 1 tsp Calum pong nut (chironjee)
- ½ inch finely chopped Ginger
- 2 -3 Finely chopped green chilies
- Finely chopped fresh coriander
- Mustard oil for frying
- 1 kg curd beaten well
- Mint green chutney
- Salt to taste
- 2 tsp Bhuna (Dry Roasted) cumin seeds
- Besan Sev
- 2 tsp red chilli powder
- 1 small bowl Sweet Tamarind chutney
- Pomegranate aril

Ingredients for Garnishing

- Tamarind sweet & sour chutney
- Fresh coriander & mint chutney
- Roasted/bhuna cumin/jeera powder
- Besan sev
- Pomegranate aril
- Red chilli powder
- Best Served with chilled beaten curd/dahi (sugar can be added to the curd).

1. Wash the dal and soak it overnight. Drain the excess water from the dal and put it into the mixer. Make a thick paste without adding water in it.
2. Take out the dal paste in a bowl and fluff-up with your hands. The mixture to make gujiya is ready.
3. Mix the chopped coconut, raisins, chironjee , chopped ginger and finely chopped green chillies & coriander together.
4. Spread a wet cloth or aluminium foil on a flat plate and put dal mix of the size of a lemon on it. Make a flat disc of 2.5 - 3 inches. Put ½ tsp nuts mixture on it and fold from one side by flipping the side of the cloth.
5. Heat mustard oil in a kadai. Fry the gujiyas on a medium flame until they turn brown from both the sides. Slide gently into the oil.
6. Whisk the curd and add salt to it.
7. Take a deep vessel and pour luke warm water into it along with salt and heeng. Now soak all the gujiyas in the water. Once they start floating in approximately 20-25 minutes take them out and gently press with hands to squeeze excess water.
8. Dip each gujiya into the curd and place on a serving plate. Spread mint coriander green chutney and sweet and sour tamarind chutney on top and Garnish with roasted cumin seeds powder, red chilli powder, black salt, pomegranate aril and besan sev.

Steamed Dahi Gujiya

- Prep time: 4 hours
- Cooking Time: 20 to 25 minutes
- Serves: 6
- Storage: Refrigerate
- Utensils Required:
- Idli stand with steamer
- Deep bowl/dish for soaking
- Deep bowl/disposable leaf bowl/dona for plating

Ingredients

- 100 gms urad dal split
- 100 gms moong dal split
- Total (1 and a half cup of dal, ratio 50:50)
- ½ inch Ginger
- 1 Green chilli
- ½ tsp salt
- 1 Eno sachet
- Pinch of Hing / Asafoetida
- Vegetable oil for greasing idli plates.
- Lukewarm water for soaking

Ingredients for the Filling

- Finely chop all the below mentioned ingredients:
- fresh green coriander,
- dry coconut,
- Raisins,
- Ginger, cashew nuts & chirounji.

Ingredients for Garnishing

- Tamarind sweet & sour chutney**(recipe below)
- fresh coriander & mint chutney **(recipe below)
- roasted/bhuna cumin/jeera powder**(recipe below)
- besan sev, pomegranate aril
- red chilli powder
- Best Served with chilled beaten curd/dahi
- (sugar can be added to the curd).

Instructions

1. Soak & rinse the dhuli moong and urad dal in water for 4 hours.
2. Grind the soaked dal in a blender with green chilli, ginger, salt & heeng to make a smooth thick batter, add very less amount of water while making the paste.
3. Finely chop all the ingredients for filling.
4. Heat the idli steamer, grease the idli plates, add ½ sachet of eno (just before pouring the batter to the idli plate).
5. Dal batter to be mixed well in one direction only.
6. Pour a spoonful of light & frothy dal batter to the idli plates, add 1 tbsp filling, again pour a spoonful of dal batter to cover the filling gently.
7. Steam for 20 mins on a medium flame.
8. Check the bhalla by inserting a fork, if it comes out clean bhalla's are done, let them cool for 5 minutes.
9. Prepare luke warm water with a pinch of hing and salt, soak the bhalla for 10-15 mins in it. Now squeeze the excess water by pressing the Bhalla gently between the hands.
10. Serve it with beaten curd and add the garnish (Tamarind chutney, green mint chutney, roasted cumin powder, red chilli powder, pomegranate arils and besan sev.

Tips/Special care

1. Curd can be sweetened with sugar/sugar free.
2. Do not skip the soaking part it helps the Bhalla to become soft and soak the flavours.
3. Do not dip for longer time just for 10 to 15 minutes.
4. Water must be Lukewarm not boiling and squeeze very gently
5. Eno to be added just before pouring the batter to the idli plate, when the steamer is ready.
6. After adding Eno mix in one direction only.
7. While pouring the batter use hand or spoon, pour in the centre 1 spoonful as it expands after cooking.
8. Use the garnish only before serving.

Sweet & Sour Tamarind Chutney

Ingredients

- 1 cup seedless tamarind
- 1 and half cup Jaggery (broken into small pieces)
- 2 tsp bhuna jeera
- 1 tsp red chilli powder
- ½ tsp Heeng
- 2 tsp black salt
- Salt to taste
- 4 tsp Raisins

Instructions

1. Soak tamarind in 4 cups of hot water for an hour.
2. Mash it using hand, strain it through soup strainer discard the pulp and keep water.
3. Add the tamarind water in a deep pan, add all the ingredients except raisins.
4. Cook on a medium heat for 15 minutes keep stirring.
5. Add raisins cook for another 15 to 20 minutes keep stirring.
6. Once it reduces, remove the pan from the heat, let it cool transfer into a glass jar.

Tip

Can be stored in the fridge for 3 to 4 months The consistency should not be very thick. Sugar or jaggery can be used as a sweetener.

Fresh Mint Coriander Chutney

- 2 cup Coriander leaves
- 1 cup Mint leaves
- ½ inch Ginger
- 4 cloves Garlic
- 1-2 Green chillies
- 2-3 tsp Lemon juice
- 1 tsp jeera
- Salt to taste

Instructions

Blend all the ingredients together in a blender to make smooth paste using very less water.
It can be made on the sil batta (stone grinding tastes good)

Tip

Few slices of Raw mango or fresh amla (gooseberry) can also be added to the chutney if in season. Decrease the amount of lemon juice if adding raw mango or amla. Store in an airtight container in the fridge.

How to make roasted cumin powder (Bhuna Jeera)

1. Heat the tawa (preferably iron tawa)
2. Dry roast the cumin seeds on a low flame for 5-10 minutes until colour of the cumin changes to dark brown
3. Let it cool, grind it and store in an airtight container.
4. Can be stored for 6 months.

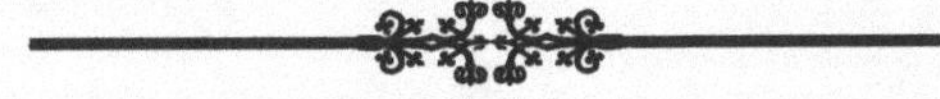

Sweet & Sour Tomato Chutney

- 4 to 5 medium sized Tomato finely chopped
- 1 medium Onion finely chopped
- 1 tbsp White vinegar
- ½ tsp Jeera
- 250 gms Sugar
- Garam masala
- 1 tbsp Oil or ghee
- Salt to taste
- ½ tsp Black pepper powder crushed
- ½ tsp red chilli powder

Instructions

1. Heat 1 teaspoon of oil in a pan on medium heat. Add finely chopped onion sauté well, then add finely chopped tomatoes.
2. Add salt, red chilli powder, black pepper crushed and garam masala. Cover and let it cook
3. Now add sugar and mix. The chutney will turn liquidy as the sugar melts. Cook for 20-25 minutes, stirring in between or until the moisture in tomatoes totally dries out. Add White vinegar and set aside.
4. Keep stirring and cook for another 2-3 minutes till it thickens a bit. Do not cook it for too long because the chutney will thicken as it cools down. Remove from heat and let it cool down. Once the chutney has cooled down, store it in an airtight container and store in the refrigerator.

Note- Adjust the garam masala and red chilli powder to taste.

Sun Dried moong dal Badi

Ingredients

- 1 kg Moong Dal split
- 2 tsp Asafoetida (hing)
- 1 tbsp red chilli powder
- 1 tbsp Garam masala (preferably homemade)
- Sunshine

Instructions

1. Soak the dal in water for 4 to 5 hours.
2. Drain all the excess water and grind without water to a coarse paste in a mixer grinder.
3. Take out the mixture in a deep utensil, add hing, red chilli powder & garam masala.
4. Beat the mixture well in one direction using hand.
5. Grease thali or trays.
6. With the help of fingers drop the dal mixture on the tray, they should be round in shape, keep distance between each vadi mixture that is dropped.
7. Once one tray is filled use another tray or thali.
8. Once all the mixture is used keep them in the sun.
9. After one day drying in the sun, the next day most of them come off easily, dry them in the sun for at least 3 to 4 days so no moisture is left.
10. Store them in an airtight container, can be stored for 6 months.
11. Can be used to make sabzi or tahri pulao.

Note

- Best time to make vadi is summertime.
- Beat the mixture well till aerated.
- Sun Dry them completely

<u>Aloo Badi Curry</u>

Prep Time: 10 minutes
Cooking Time: 20 minutes
Serves:4
Utensils required: Pressure cooker
For Plating: Serving Bowl

Ingredients

- ½ cup dried Moong Dal Badi
- 2 tbsp Desi Ghee
- 1 tsp Asafoetida (Heeng)
- 1 tsp cumin seeds (Jeera)
- 2 potatoes cut then into cubes
- 1 onion paste
- 2 tomato puree
- 1 small green chilli chopped
- 1/2 tsp red chilli powder
- ½ tsp Turmeric powder
- Salt to taste
- ½ tsp Garam masala
- ½ tsp Coriander powder
- 2 cups of water
- Fresh coriander finely chopped for garnishing

Instructions

1. In a pressure cooker heat 2 tbsp ghee on a low flame add half cup dried mangodi to fry, shallow fry it until it becomes golden brown, take it out.
2. In the same oil add ½ tsp heeng, ½ tsp Jeera, onion paste sauté, add tomato puree let it cook add turmeric powder, red chilli powder, coriander powder, salt to taste ,chopped green chilli, garam masala powder cook the masala , then add fried mangodi and potatoes sauté for a minute add 2 to 2 and a half cups of water.
3. Close the lid of the pressure cooker, let it cook on high flame till 1 whistle then lower the flame and let it cook for 5 to 7 mins.

Note

Mangodi's usually soak the water. Adjust the water according to the gravy consistency required it can be thin or thick gravy as per preference.
You can also add a tsp of desi ghee while serving.
Enjoy with roti, paratha, or rice.

Kade masale Kathal do Pyaza

Prep time: 20 minutes
Cooking time: 30 minutes
Serves: 4
Utensils Required
Heavy bottomed iron kadai
For Plating: serving bowl

Ingredients

- 1 kg Kathal (Raw Jack fruit peeled, cut into cubes)
- 1 kg sliced onion
- Garam masala (3 to 4 black cardamom, 3 to 4 bay leaves, cinnamon stick, 8 cloves, 1 tsp jeera, 5 to 6 whole red chillies)
- Mustard oil
- ½ tsp turmeric powder
- 2 to 3 tsp coriander powder
- 2 tsp deggi mirch
- 2 large tomatoes chopped
- ½ cup curd
- Salt to taste

Instructions

1. In an iron kadai heat mustard oil, add the garam masala once fragrant, add the jack fruit cubes sauté till reddish brown.
2. Add finely sliced onions, sauté both kathal and onions on a low flame for 5 to 7 minutes.
3. Now add the tomatoes, dry masala, salt, curd, saute for 10 minutes.
4. Cover and cook well till done. Finally, sauté it for another 5 minutes
5. Garnish with freshly chopped coriander.
6. Serve hot with roti, rice or dosa.

Besan ki machli (Veg Fish)

Prep time: 20 minutes
Cooking time: 30 minutes
Serves: 4
Utensils Required
Heavy bottomed kadai or pan
For Plating: serving bowl

Ingredients For the besan 'fillets'

- ½ cup besan
- ¼ tsp turmeric
- ½ tsp red chilli powder
- ¼ tsp ajwain
- ¼ tsp jeera
- ½ tsp Heeng
- Salt to taste
- 2 cups water

For the curry

- _Mustard oil_
- _3 medium sized finely sliced Onion_
- _2 Tomato puree_
- _Ginger garlic paste_
- _1 tbsp Meethi daana_
- _2 Bay leaves_
- _3 to 4 Cloves_
- _2 Black cardamom_
- _1 small Cinnamon stick_
- _1 tbsp curd_
- _1 tsp deggi red chilli powder_
- _1 tsp Turmeric powder_
- _2 tsp Coriander powder_
- _½ tsp Garam masala_
- _pinch of heeng_
- _Salt to taste_

Instructions

1. In a deep bowl take ½ cup besan, ¼ tsp turmeric, ½ tsp red chilli powder, salt, now coarsely grind ¼ tsp ajwain, a pinch or two Heeng, ¼ tsp jeera in mortar pestle or mixer grinder.
2. 2. Add 2 t cups of water, whisk well, and prepare a watery batter.
3. Pour the batter into a heavy bottomed kadai or pan, cook on a medium flame stirring continuously, until it thickens and leaves the pan. Prepare a plate or thali by greasing it with few drops of mustard oil.
4. Transfer the thickened mixture immediately over the plate and spread uniformly.
5. Allow it to cool completely. Cut into diamond shape or a shape of your choice.

For the curry

1. In a kadai, heat mustard oil for shallow or deep frying the besan fillets. The besan fillets can be air fried also.
2. In another pan or kadai add mustard oil, add a pinch of heeng, meethi seeds, jeera, bay leaves, black cardamom, cinnamon, cloves and cook for a minute until fragrant.
3. Add finely sliced onions, let them brown, add ginger garlic paste, tomato puree and cook for a minute. Add deggi mirch, coriander powder, turmeric powder, 1 tbsp curd and salt to taste, let it cook, till oil separates. Now add 1 to 2 cups of water bring the gravy to a boil. Slide the besan fillets gently.
4. Simmer for 5 minutes until the flavours are absorbed well.
5. Finally add freshly chopped coriander.
6. Serve it hot with Steamed rice, roti or dosa.

<u>***Makhani Gravy***</u>

- 10 to 12 roughly chopped tomatoes
- 10 to 12 Broken cashew nuts
- 2 to 3 tsp fresh cream
- 2 tsp butter
- 2 -3 tsp oil
- 2 to 3 tsp Kasuri meethi (dried fenugreek leaves)
- 2 roughly chopped onion
- 2 whole red chilli
- 3 tsp honey
- Garlic cloves 7-8 chopped
- Ginger 1 tsp chopped
- 5 to 6 green cardamoms
- Salt to taste
- 2 tsp Deggi mirch powder
- 2 tsp dhania powder
- 1 black cardamom
- 1 tsp Jeera
- ½ blade Mace
- 2 cloves

Instructions

1. This gravy can be used for making butter chicken, shahi paneer or a malai kofta
2. Heat oil in a heavy bottomed pan add jeera, mace, cloves, black cardamom, green cardamom sauté, add ginger garlic sauté for a minute.
3. Add roughly chopped tomatoes, broken cashews, salt, dhania powder, deggi mirch powder & add a cup of water cover let it cook for 10 minutes on a low flame.
4. Finally add kasuri methi, butter honey. let it cook for 5 minutes.
5. Let it cool and grind it in a blender little water can be used while grinding, strain the gravy thru a strainer (do not skip this) for a creamy/ makhmali gravy.
6. Warm the gravy add cream check the seasoning.
7. Pour the gravy into the serving bowl, add the koftas, paneer tikka, roasted chicken or palak paneer koftas place it on the gravy immediately.

Tastes best with lachha parantha , tandoori roti, Naan.

<u>*Green Egg Curry*</u>

Prep time: 20 minutes
Cooking Time: 20 minutes
Serves: 4
Utensils Required: Deep Kadai or Pan, spatula for cooking
For Plating: Serving Bowl or deep dish

Ingredients list

- Green masala paste
- Green chilli 1 (can be adjusted according to taste)
- A bunch of fresh green coriander
- 4 to 5 leaves of fresh mint
- 2 tsp lemon juice
- 6 whole boiled eggs (peeled)
- 2 medium onion paste
- 2 tsp ginger- garlic paste
- 2 tspDhania powder
- ½ tsp Garam masala powder
- ½ tsp Deggi Mirch
- 2 Bay leaf
- 2 cloves
- 1 black cardamom
- 1 small stick cinnamon
- 2 green cardamoms
- ½ tsp jeera
- 2 to 3 tsp Fresh cut Meethi or Kasuri Meethi
- Fresh cream 2 tsp
- Oil 2 to 3 tsp
- Salt to taste

Instructions

1. Boil the whole eggs, peel them & slit them vertically but do not slice the eggs.
2. Heat the oil in a kadai, add whole garam masala let them sizzle, add jeera than onion paste, let it cook on medium heat
3. Add the ginger-garlic paste sauté
4. Add dhania powder, salt, deggi mirch powder if using fresh meethi cook along the masala
5. Add green masala, let it cook for 3-4 mins
6. Once the masala is cooked add boiled eggs, garam masala & fresh cream, switch off the heat.

Tastes best with roti, laccha parantha or steamed rice

<u>*Sil batta Masala chicken curry*</u>

Prep time: 15 minutes
Cooking time: 30 minutes
Serves: 4
Utensils Required
Heavy bottomed kadai or pan
For Plating: serving bowl

<u>*Ingredients*</u>

- 1 kg chicken (washed and marinated in salt and turmeric powder)
- Mustard oil
- ½ cup Curd
- 1 large tomato
- 2 Bay leaves
- Salt to taste
- 1 tsp Jeera
- 3 to 4 Onion finely chopped
- Fresh coriander finely chopped
- Sil batta (Natural stone mortar for grinding)

For the sil batta masala (Grind all together using water on the sil batta)

- 8 to 9 Garlic cloves
- 1 inch ginger
- Whole red chillies 4 to 5
- Whole black pepper 5 to 6
- 4 to 5 cloves
- 1 stick cinnamon
- 2 black cardamoms
- 4 green cardamoms
- 1 tsp cumin seeds
- 2 tsp Whole coriander seeds
- ½ nutmeg
- 1 Mace
- Fresh Turmeric small root
- A pinch of salt while grinding

Instructions

1. In a heavy bottom kadai, add mustard oil, let it smoke, add jeera, bay leaves and finely chopped onions sauté, let them brown.
2. Now add the freshly grinded sil batta masala, saute for 3 to 4 minutes, add chopped tomato once soft, add the marinated chicken sauté for 5 minutes, add curd and sauté for another 10 minutes.
3. Once the chicken leaves oil add 1 cup water, cover and let it cook for 5 to 10 minutes.
4. Once cooked garnish with freshly chopped coriander leaves.
5. Serve hot with rice, roti, paratha or dosa.

Mutton stew

Prep time: 15 minutes
Cooking time: 20 minutes
Serves: 4
Storage: Refrigerate (can be stored for 2 days)
Utensils Required
Pressure cooker
For Plating: serving bowl

Ingredients

- 1 kg mutton (Goat pieces from leg and shoulder)
- 1.25 kg finely sliced red onions
- ½ kg Curd whisked
- 4 to 5 Whole dry red chillies
- 3 to 4 Green chillies whole
- ½ tsp Turmeric powder
- Salt to taste
- 2 to 3 tbsp Whole Coriander seeds
- 3 to 4 tbsp Finely chopped ginger garlic

Whole garam masala

- 6-7 cloves
- 10-12 black peppercorns
- 2 black cardamoms
- 2 green cardamoms
- 1 inch piece of cinnamon stick
- 1 mace flower
- ¼ nutmeg
- 2 tbsp Rice bran oil
- 2 tbsp Desi ghee

Instructions

1. In a pressure cooker add oil and ghee, first fry 1.25 kg finely sliced onions, take them out once transparent, and keep aside for later use.
2. In the same oil now add the mutton sauté well while adding 4 to 5 tsp of curd. (keep the remaining curd for later use).
3. Add all the whole spices, whole coriander seeds, whole red chillies, whole green chillies, finely chopped ginger garlic, turmeric powder, and salt to taste sauté for some time and pressure cook for around 10 mins on a low flame after one whistle.
4. The mutton should be ¾ cooked not fully as it must sautéed later.
5. Open the pressure cooker lid and sauté by adding fried transparent onions.
6. Keep adding the remaining curd while sauteing on a medium flame.
7. Once the oil separates and the mutton is fully cooked, garnish it with freshly chopped green coriander.
8. Serve hot with a roti or paratha.

Mutton Chops

Prep time: 15 minutes
Cooking time: 20 minutes
Serves: 4
Storage: Refrigerate (can be stored for 2 to 3 days)
Utensils Required
Pressure cooker and Tawa nonstick
For Plating: serving platter or tray

Ingredients

- 1 kg mutton chops
- 4 lemon juice
- 1 tbsp Black pepper freshly crushed
- Salt to taste
- 3 to 4 tbsp Ginger garlic paste
- 2 tbsp oil
- White butter for shallow frying

Instructions

1. In a pressure cooker add 2 tbsp oil. Add ginger garlic paste. Let it cook.
2. Add washed and clean mutton chops.
3. Cook for some time then add salt, crushed black pepper and lemon juice. Cook for 2 to 3 minutes.
4. Now add little water pressure cook for 10 to 15 minutes.
5. Open the pressure cooker, check if it is cooked well, and dry the water completely.
6. Shallow fry on a tawa using white butter or air fry the chops in an airfryer.
7. Serve it with green mint coriander chutney.

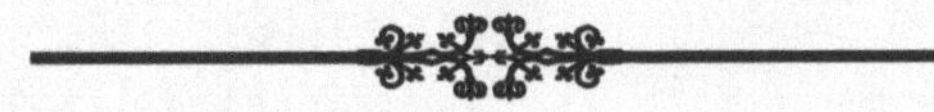

Tahri - Matar, Gajjar, Gobhi , Aloo, fresh Methi leaves
(Winter Special one pot meal during Lunch)

Prep time: 20 minutes
Cooking time: 30 minutes
Serves: 4
Utensils Required
Heavy bottomed kadai or pan
For Plating: serving rice plate

Ingredients

- ½ cup Fresh or frozen peas
- ½ cup Carrots
- ½ cup Chopped Cauliflower florets
- ½ cup Fresh methi leaves
- 2 large Potato cut in cubes
- 3 medium sized finely sliced onions
- 2 medium sized chopped Tomato
- Whole spices (2 Bay leaves, 1 tsp Jeera, 2 black cardamom and 1 stick cinnamon)
- 3 tbsp Desi ghee
- 1.5 cups Long grained basmati rice (washed and soaked for 30 minutes)
- 1 tsp Turmeric powder
- ½ tsp red chilli powder
- ½ tsp coriander powder
- Salt to taste
- 2 green chillies slit
- 3 cups water

Instructions

1. In a heavy- bottomed kadai, heat ghee and add finely sliced onions, fry till golden brown.
2. Add the whole spices and stir-fry till they release their aroma.
3. Now add the fresh peas, cauliflower florets, potato cubes, sliced carrots, slit green chillies, fresh Methi leaves and sauté for a minute or 2.
4. Add chopped tomatoes let it cook for a minute, add all the dry masalas red chilli powder, coriander powder, turmeric powder, and salt to taste. Mix well
5. Drain the rice. Add to the kadai, stir fry for a minute, till the ghee coats.
6. Add water cover and cook till the rice is cooked for 10 minutes on a low flame.
7. Serve hot with green mint and coriander chutney freshly made on sil batta or mixer grinder, papad, raita and achar.

Green Moong Dal Chilla

It is a healthy protein packed and tasty option for breakfast or any meal.

Prep time: overnight soaking of dal
Cooking time: 20 minutes
Serves: 2
Storage: Refrigerate (dal can be stored for 2 days)
Utensils Required
Non-Stick tawa or cast-iron tawa
For Plating: serving plate

Ingredients

- 1 cup Whole green moong dal
- 1 tbsp Finely chopped onion
- 1 tbsp Finely chopped red bell pepper
- 1 tbsp Fresh coriander finely chopped
- 1 tbsp Grated carrots
- 1 tbsp Grated beetroot
- 1 tbsp Grated Cottage cheese
- 1 chilli green chillies
- Salt to taste
- ½ tsp Black pepper
- ½ tsp amchoor powder
- Pinch of Heeng
- A pinch of red chilli powder
- ½ tsp Chaat masala
- Few drops Ghee or vegetable oil

Instructions

1. Soak the whole green moong dal overnight with enough water.
2. Discard the soaked water, wash the dal thoroughly.
3. Grind the moong dal adding little water in the blender to a smooth consistency.
4. The batter should neither be too thick nor too thin.
5. Add onion, green chillies, bell pepper, salt, black pepper, amchur powder, pinch of turmeric & Heeng, fresh coriander and red chilli powder mix well.
6. Heat the nonstick tawa, take the ladleful of batter, pour in the centre, and spread. Cook on both sides using little ghee.
7. For the filling mix grated carrots, grated beetroot, and cottage cheese, add chaat masala and salt.
8. Serve hot with curd and mint chutney.

Note Chilla can be made with any other dal, split moong dal, split masoor dal or besan.

Moong Dal mangodi ki sabzi (Fresh or Sundried moong dal Badi)

Prep Time 2 to 3 hour (Including soaking of dal)
Cooking Time 30 minutes
Serves 4
Utensils required Heavy bottomed kadai or pan
For Plating Serving Bowl

Mangodi Ki Sabzi

Ingredients For Mangodi

- ½ cup yellow split moong dal
- a pinch asafoetida (Heeng)
- salt, to taste
- Red chilli powder
- Mustard oil, for frying
- For tadka
- Fenugreek seeds (Methi seeds)
- Asafoetida (Heeng)
- Jeera Instructions

For gravy

- 1 onion, chopped
- 2 tomatoes, chopped
- 1 green chilli, chopped
- 1 tbsp ginger finely chopped
- 1 tsp red chilli powder
- 1/2 tsp turmeric powder
- 1 tsp Coriander powder
- Water for thin gravy
- salt, to taste

Instructions

1. Soak the moong dal in 4 cups of water for about 2 to 3 hours.
2. Drain the soaked dal of all the extra water and grind the dal along with asafoetida and salt in the mixer jar. Blend to a coarse paste. Add little water as required for grinding. Do not add a lot of water otherwise it will not form dumplings. Beat the mixture well till aerated.
3. Heat mustard oil in a small deep heavy bottomed kadai. Add Spoonfuls of lentil paste and deep fry until golden on a medium flame. Remove on an absorbent kitchen towel.
4. Heat mustard oil in another pan. Once the oil is hot, add Heeng, Methi seeds, jeera once it splutters add the chopped onions and green chillies. Reserve some green chilli for garnish.
5. Sauté for a minute and then add the ginger. Cook for 2-3 minutes till the onions start to soften. Add the tomatoes and all the spices. Mix well and cook covered for 5 mins.
6. Add about 4 cup water for thin gravy. Stir until there is a boil. Reduce heat and cook until you get the desired consistency of the thin gravy.
7. Add the fried dal mangodi and cook covered for another 5 mins. You may also keep some of the mangodi's as is to serve on the side.
8. Garnish with green coriander and serve hot with Paranths or rice.

Notes

- You can also add a tsp of desi ghee while serving.
- You can also use red lentils or whole green moong dal. Any lentil of your choice will work, just remember some lentils may need longer soaking time.
- Dal can be grinded coarsely on a sil batta or mixer

Kachche keema ke kofte

Prep time: 20 minutes
Cooking Time: 35 minutes
Marination Time: - 3 to 4 hours
Serves: 4
Utensils Required: Deep heavy bottomed Kadai or Pan, spatula for cooking
For Plating: Serving Bowl or deep dish

Ingredients For Koftas

- Mutton mince (Keema)
- 3 to 4 tsp Ginger-garlic Paste
- 1 tsp Green Chilli Paste
- Green chillies, chopped
- Fresh coriander leaves, chopped
- 3 to 4 tsp Dry Coconut paste (coconut powder & water mix into a smooth paste)
- 3 to 4 tsp Poppy seeds paste (soak it in water for half an hour than make a smooth paste)
- Black Pepper
- Salt

For Binding the Kofta
- 1 egg
- 9 to 10 tsp Roasted Chana powder

For Kofta Filling

- Chopped Green Chillies, Fresh Coriander, Raisin & Chironji(Charoli)

For the Gravy

- 2 kgs onions sliced
- 3 to 4 tsp Ginger-garlic paste
- Salt
- dry coriander powder, red chilli powder
- Turmeric powder half a tsp (a pinch or two as the gravy should not look yellow in colour)
- Garam Masala powder,
- 4 to 5 Bay Leaves
- 6 to 7 cloves.

<u>***Method***</u>

Step1- Marinate the mutton mince with 3 to 4 tsp ginger- garlic paste &1 tsp green chilli paste, salt to taste, chopped green chilli, chopped green coriander, 3 to 4 tsp poppy seed paste & 3 to 4 tsp dry coconut paste for at least 4 to 5 hours. After marination for Binding add 1 egg & Roasted Chana powder in the mince.

Step2- Make small round portions, now flatten each portion & add the filling (4 raisin, 4 Chironji, pinch of green chilli & fresh coriander chopped) in each round portion. keep the filled koftas for 20 mins on a side so it dries a bit.

Step3- For gravy in a heavy bottom kadai add vegetable oil, bay leaves, cloves, black cardamom, green cardamom, jeera 1 tsp, add sliced onions. Once the onion becomes transparent lower the flame & put koftas on the top of onions, cover the lid so the steam lets the koftas cook (Do not stir at all at this stage) for at least 10 mins.

Now check if the koftas have hardened then stir gently, let the onions mash up a bit so the gravy becomes thick, add ginger-garlic paste 3 to 4 tsp, red chilli powder, dry coriander powder, salt, pinch or two of turmeric powder, garam masala powder, black pepper powder, let it cook on a low flame.

As the oil separates, add 4 to 5 tsp poppy seeds paste & 3 to 4 tsp coconut paste stir gently, let it cook. If required, add some water.

Garnish it with Freshly chopped Coriander.

Note: For people who do not like a sweet taste can add 4 to 5 tsp curd.

Here's My Grandmother's Yummiest Mutton Kofta Recipe!!!

<u>*Mutton or Chicken Yakhni Pulao*</u>

- Prep time: 20-25 minutes
- Cooking time: 30 minutes
- Serves: 4
- Utensils Required
- Heavy bottomed kadai or pan
- For Plating: serving rice plate

Ingredients For the Bouquet Garni

- 2 to 3 tbsp Saunf (Fennel)
- 3 to 4 tbsp whole coriander seeds
- 1 large onion cut
- 6 cloves
- 5 to 6 black peppers
- 6 to 7 Green cardamom
- 2 Black cardamom
- 2 bay leaves
- 1 tsp jeera
- 1 pod Garlic
- 1 inch Ginger

For the yakhni

500 gms -mutton goat curry cut or 1 small chicken (if preparing mutton yakhni pressure, cook it.
If preparing Chicken yakhni, less cooking time is required use an open pan).
4 cups water
1 tsp salt

For the Pulao

- 500 gms long grained basmati rice washed and soaked
- 3 to 4 tbsp ghee
- 1 tsp jeera
- 4 to 5 black peppers
- 4 green cardamoms
- 2 black cardamoms
- 3 to 4 green chillies slit
- 2 bay leaves
- Red chilli powder to taste
- 1 tbsp Coriander powder
- ½ cup curd
- 3 medium sized finely sliced onions
- 1 tbsp ginger garlic paste
- Salt to taste (use little salt as already used in yakhni)
- 2 to 3 drops Kewra water
- Few strands of kesar soaked in milk
- 1 tbsp Garam masala

Instructions

1. Prepare the bouquet garni in a muslin cloth or cheesecloth by adding all the ingredients and tying it up.
2. Add 500 gms mutton, bouquet garni, 4 cups water and salt to pressure cook for 15 minutes. Let the pressure release naturally.
3. Remove the bouquet garni with tongs. Strain the mutton and stock through a strainer, reserving the mutton and stock (yakhni) separately. Squeeze out all the juices from the bouquet garni into the stock.
4. In a separate kadai or pan add ghee, add all the whole spices, sauté for a minute until fragrant. Add finely sliced onions sauté till golden brown.
5. Add ginger garlic paste sauté, add boiled mutton pieces, add red chilli powder, coriander powder, and little salt as yakhni (stock) already has salt in it. Sauté for 2 to 3 minutes add curd sauté for another 5 minutes
6. Add washed basmati rice, garam masala powder, reserved yakhni stock, kewra drops, kesar strands. Cover and cook on a low flame for 10 minutes, till the rice is fully cooked.
7. Serve the rice with a layer of brown onion fresh finely chopped coriander.
8. Serve hot with raita and mint -coriander chutney.

Bharwan keema karela

Prep time: 15 minutes
Cooking time: 20 minutes
Serves: 4
Storage: Refrigerate (can be stored for 2 to 3 days)
Utensils Required
Heavy bottomed kadai or pan
For Plating: serving bowl or tray

Ingredients

- Small even sized green Karela (bitter gourd)
- Mutton keema
- Ginger- garlic paste
- Tomato
- Chopped onion
- Mustard oil
- Saunf (fennel)
- Deggi mirch
- Coriander powder
- Amchoor powder
- Salt to taste
- Onions finely sliced
- White thread (to tie the karelas)
- Preparation time 30 mins
- Cooking time 25 mins
- Serves 2

Ingredients

- 10-12 mini karela/bitter gourd
- salt to taste
- ½ tsp turmeric
- 1 tbsp oil
- For Stuffing:
- 1 tbsp oil
- 1 tsp cumin seeds
- 1 green chili, sliced
- ½ tsp red chili powder
- 1 tsp sugar
- 1 tbsp garlic ginger, chopped
- 3 tbsps onion, chopped
- ½ cup soy keema (minced soya), water as required, clean cotton thread for binding.

Method

1. Scrape the bitter gourd and save the scraped skin. Slit in the middle and de-seed.
2. Apply salt and turmeric to the bitter gourd and allow to rest for 30 minutes to reduce its bitterness.
3. For the stuffing, heat oil in a pan, add cumin seeds, garlic, ginger, and green chilies. Sauté till light pink.
4. Add soy keema, scraped karela skin, red chili powder and mix well. Add little water if needed. Check for salt and add sugar to balance the bitterness. Let the mixture cook for 5-7 minutes remove and let it cool.
5. Stuff this mixture into the slit bitter gourds and bind them carefully with cotton threads.
6. Shallow fry in a little oil until bitter gourds are cooked evenly.
7. Serve immediately.

<u>*Meethe Pue*</u>

This dish is usually made during festivals on karvachauth or Ahoi Ashtami

Prep time: 10 minutes
Cooking time: 5 minutes
Serves: 4
Utensils Required
Kadai or pan for frying
For Plating: serving plate

Ingredients

- 1 cup whole wheat flour
- ½ cup Jaggery or sugar
- 1 tsp green cardamom powder
- 1 tsp Fennel coarsely crushed
- Oil for frying
- Water as required

Instructions

1. In a bowl, take whole wheat flour, add sugar, and fennel seeds powder. Mix with a spoon.
2. Add water in small quantity till flowing consistency, mix with spoon. Ensure no lumps are formed.
3. Rest the batter for 10 minutes. Meanwhile, heat the oil for frying the pue. After 10 minutes whisk the batter in one direction. The batter is ready.
4. For testing the hotness of oil, put a drop like quantity from the batter. If bubbles form on the pue sides, the oil is ready for frying.
5. With the help of a spoon or with your hands pour a small portion of the batter. Fry the pue from all sides till they are brown in colour.
6. Meethe Pue is ready to serve. Serve it with rice kheer or with tea.

Note

Coarsely grind the fennel seeds to make its powder for adding in the batter. You can add elaichi/cardamom powder and baking soda to the batter to make them fluffy and soft, if you want. Whisking the batter in one direction makes the pue soft and fluffy.

Makhane ki kheer

This sweet dessert is made during Navratri fasting, Mahashivratri or Ekadashi fasting.

Prep time: 15 minutes
Cooking time: 20 minutes
Serves: 4
Utensil required: heavy bottomed kadai or pan

Ingredients

- 1 cup Phool makhana/ fox nut
- 2 cup whole milk
- 1 tbsp green cardamom powder
- 3 to 4 tbsp Sugar or Sweetener of your choice
- 3 tsp Desi ghee (clarified buter)
- 1 pinch saffron
- 1 tbsp chironji
- 1 tbsp raisins
- 1 tbsp Sliced almonds

Instructions

- Heat ghee in a pan, add phool makhana and roast them on a low flame, till they become crunchy.
- Grind half makhana in a mixer to make a powder, reserve the rest makhanas.
- Heat milk in a thick and heavy bottomed pan on a low to medium heat. Let the milk come to boil.
- Add the makhana powder and remaining whole roasted makhana in the boiling milk, let it simmer on a medium flame till the milk thickens and makhanas soften for 10 minutes.
- Add sugar and saffron, let it cook. Once it thickens add cardamom powder and raisins.
- Garnish with sliced almonds, raisins and chironji.
- Can be served warm or chilled.

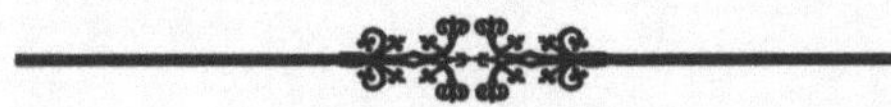

<u>*Lauki ka halwa*</u>

Prep time: 10 minutes
Cooking time: 30 minutes
Serves: 3 to 4
Utensils required: heavy bottomed kadai or pan

Ingredients

- 600 gms grated Lauki (Bottle Gourd) Do not grate the seeds
- ½ cup milk
- 1 tbsp khoya
- ½ cup sugar or jaggery or sugar free (as per choice)
- ¼ tsp green cardamom powder
- 1 tbsp almonds sliced
- 1 tbsp pistachio sliced
- Edible silver leaf/ varak
- 3 tbsp desi ghee (clarified butter)

Instructions

1. Grate the bottle gourd without seeds and sauté in ghee on low flame. Do not grate the bottle gourd and keep as it changes the colour. Sauté for 10 minutes until the moisture dries completely.
2. Add the milk and cook on a medium to low flame till the milk thickens. Add the sugar cook for 3 to 4 minutes till it thickens and dries
3. Add khoya, cardamom powder and 1 tbsp ghee let it mix well for a minute.
4. Garnish it with sliced almonds, pistachio, dry Gulab leaves and silver varak. It can be served warm or chilled.

Gratitude

Gurur Brahma Gurur Vishnu Gurur Devo Maheshwarar,
Guru Sakshat Parabrahma Tasmai Shri Guruve Namaha...

In Sanskrit Guru means **Gu**-Darkness **Ru**-remover of ignorance darkness.
Thank you to all my mentors/ Gurus for bringing in the light.

Food mentors my grandmother **PremLata,** my uncle **Ajit Kumar Singh Retd. Joint Director Tourism Uttrakhand** & my entire loving **family.**

To my wonderful mom **Santosh Singh** who has put her feet in dads shoe's after he passed away.

To the most progressive men in my life Dad **Late Shri Vijay Kumar**,
husband **Ashish** & my son **Neil.**

Sa Vidya ya vimuktaye ..

The motto of my college which means it is truly education that liberates.
To my college **'Lady Shri Ram college'.**

Elsa sisterhood (the alumni association of my college), especially **Bangalore Chapter.**

To my Dance mentors **Anika & Roma.**

To my younger Sister **Sunanda** who always promised to help me in the kitchen at 2.00 am to cook, praising me as the world's best cook. but would appear only once food was ready. To the moments of togetherness, to be cherished forever...

To marvellous **Dr. Aditi Govitrikar** for encouraging me to write a book and being my mentor in this Journey of Pageantry!

To my rampwalk mentor **Nayanika chatterjee** in this journey from food to heels!

To **God** and **Mother earth**, my heart is filled with only gratitude!

Thank you everyone for making me find my right balance and right Ingredients

Whether in life or food!